DIRECTIONS

Real Organizational Improvements

ERIK N. BOE

Dedication

I dedicate this book to my colleagues who worked with me in the hardware group at Apple. During a transformational time for the company, we were able to move the group forward to face demands of a new area. By using the steps outlined in this book, we helped turn the company away from the abyss toward a future brighter than anyone could have imagined.

Contents

Preface

I started my career at Apple in the international software group. One of our goals was to make one release of the computer operating system support many languages. At the time, it was common practice to ship the English version first and localized versions later (sometimes more than a year later). In order to achieve simultaneous release, it quickly became clear that we had to present convincing information consistently throughout the company. We needed to create a model for making decisions about what languages to support, accounting for investments and returns. Ever since, I have approached complicated decisions in large groups by creating models, making it possible to speak a common language. The elements of the operational model became clear to me after years of experimentation. It is my hope that this book will make you successful in implementing your own operational model. It is not the concepts themselves that are the biggest challenge, but rather, balancing the implementation against the everyday demands of a fast-moving organization. This book shows you how to break the challenge into small, manageable steps and lay them out over time. In doing so, it becomes a model in itself for how to engage the organization in setting directions.

Acknowledgments

I would like to thank my manager at Apple, Jackie Streeter. In partnership, we implemented and validated the concepts in this book. I would also like to thank my managers at Adobe, Frits Habermann, and Ranjit Desai, whom I worked with for years. Their trust and support in the concept made the group operate like clockwork amid many challenging transformations. Finally, I would like to thank my manager at VMware, Dale Ferrario, for supporting my work building operational models for developing and delivering complex software systems.

1

Why Do You Need Directions?

What is a company, a firm, an enterprise, a business? The origin of the word "business" comes from the idea of being busy, doing socially valuable and rewarding work. A company is formed around getting something done. It fills a gap, it solves a problem. If done well, a company can change the world.

You can buy a company. You can sell a company. A company may be involved in selling products. A company must operate within the law. A company can own things that you can track down, such as a store or a website. A company can label its offices. It has an address. A company pays employees to represent it. Employees must be offered rights as outlined by the law. Customers expect to be treated fairly and be protected from wrongdoings. A company has partners and suppliers. And a company has an owner or a group who cares for its well-being.

Having said all of this, a company is still just a concept. It is not something that you can pick up and hold. What makes one company significantly different from another is its core beliefs as manifested by its behavior. Or, in other words, its operational model. An operational model is the collective behavior of everyone who comes in contact with the company. The four major groups forming a company are employees, partners, stakeholders, and customers.

You could argue what really sets companies apart is their products and services, or the industries they are serving. Yes, that is correct if you are looking at what a company delivers to customers or society. If you're focusing on what makes an organization produce magnificent outcomes, however, it's not the end product that is the most important. It is the people behind it. And because people are behind every product ever produced, the focus has to be on how they make this happen.

It is my belief that a great operational model is the embodiment of a successful company. I am not arguing that a model alone will produce success. I am saying that having an operational model that is managed and focused on a company's purpose will produce better results. And since you already are running a company, a group, or are building one, why would you not make your operational model the best it can be?

One Versus All

We all know that one person can make a difference. The right person at the right time can change the direction of humankind. History comes alive through people's amazing adventures. Innovations spring from individuals with terrific ideas. Who among us does not know about Edison and the light bulb? Or the Wright brothers and human flight? Or Madame Curie, who was a pioneer in discovering radioactivity? They were among the many who brought our civilization to where it is today. And there were many more like them, and many more will follow in their footsteps.

When reading about past explorers, we sometimes skim over the time and place where they lived. Edison didn't simply wake up one day and invent the light bulb. He employed a large staff of highly educated scientists who worked endless hours testing out different ways of constructing a light bulb. He was an inventor and an entrepreneur—a businessperson.

Making human flight possible was a societal effort. The technology available at that time, the educational system, the banking industry, and more all played a role. The first fixed-wing aircraft was conceived and flown a hundred years before the Wright brothers made their first flight. They built a test facility to perfect the idea of controlling an airplane in three dimensions. And they became the first to make it possible to control an airplane in the air. Their invention helped change the direction of humankind. But they could not have done it alone. They stood atop the collective effort of people around and before them.

When running a company or managing a large group, investing in amazing individuals is one criterion required for success. However, the most important thing is to establish an operational model that allows all employees to contribute at their maximum potential. Their collective effort will change the course of a company. If this was not the case, why do we need a company? Why don't we just allow one or two amazing people to take care of business?

If you want to expand, grow, and create new products and services, then you need to hire employees. You need the support of other people. Everyone you hire should be exceptional in some way. But an amazing group of people is not enough. It requires a methodology. It demands a set of rules and behaviors focused on something. Make that something the company purpose. A purpose gives a group a reason for working together. The better the group is at coordinating and collaborating, the better the results.

It is not where you are today that matters. It is not what an individual knows or can do today that makes a difference. It is their desire to grow, learn, and become better that matters. An organization can change, improve, and excel if its collective belief is that growth is possible everywhere, every day. Therefore, hire people who have the skills you need, and challenge them to grow. Hire people who have the desire to make an impact on the world. These are the people who collectively will perform much better than any small group of individuals.

Haves Versus Have-Nots

Does every company have an operational model? What if all employees did whatever they wanted at any given time? It might be chaotic, but that is your operational model. Just because it changes frequently does not mean you don't have a model. A model should change over time to meet changing demands, but that change should have purpose and direction.

A leader may say a company is agile, responding to needs as they arise. A manager may allow teams to do their own things to accommodate different personalities and situations. Still, the collective effort is the operational model. In short, if there is a company, it will have one or more operational models. If not, you do not have a company. Without one, all you have is people staring at each other and wondering what to do next.

The classic argument against creating an operational model is that flexibility—the ability to respond to changes—is very important. To be successful, one must take advantage of the changing environment. One cannot afford to make long-term plans because of shifting needs and priorities. As a result, any model is rejected because it is seen as a hindrance to success. I believe there is no conflict here between flexibility (less structure) and an operational model (more structure) that is focused on getting results.

Let me illustrate my point. How do you spend your weekends? Do you get things done? Are you able to get out there and enjoy life? Do you go to new and interesting restaurants? Did you go to a nearby town to explore? Or do you end up at home in front of the computer? If you are like me, it will vary. Some weekends nothing seems to happen, while others are just too busy.

Do you make plans, or do you wait and see what happens? If it's the latter, you are flexible and can do whatever you want. If someone stops by, you will have to time to hang out. If there is a new movie released, you can go and see it. If someone sends you an invitation for a last-minute party, you go.

Or do you plan ahead? Do you spend time mapping out your weekends? If you take this approach, you may make hotel and dinner reservations ahead of time. If you wanted to hang out with friends, you told them—and perhaps even invited them over before the weekend started. Some events will change, and some of the plans may fall through. It also means that you are less able to respond to last-minute changes. Regardless, compare these two approaches, and ask yourself these questions: Which one accomplishes the most? Which path will give you a more rewarding weekend?

A group of people asked themselves these very questions. They did a study on it where they compared the approach taken by planners versus nonplanners in making weekends the most productive and fun. The result: the planners accomplished more, and felt their weekends were more fun. It turned out that being flexible and going with the flow just did not offer them as many choices. Things didn't just happen. Getting things done at the last minute takes time. Perhaps the restaurant did not allow walk-ins, or the lines were an hour long. Perhaps your friends were gone for the weekend and you could not hang out with them. Without a plan, the nonplanners felt less urgency about getting things done. Hence, they had less fun and accomplished less. The planners had an approach to their weekend; they had a plan. They set aside time to think about and prepare for fun events before they happened.

What makes a company successful? In most industries everyone wants to be ahead of the competition. Therefore, a company must be able to respond to changes quickly. This is often done by becoming agile, allowing employees to change their focus and goals as needed. Must a company constantly change in order to stay ahead? Research has shown that companies that believed in their own timeless principles did better. Refer to the book *Great by Choice* by Jim Collins. They spent less time worrying about the competition. Instead they invested in operational models that embodied their beliefs, regardless of ups and downs. Constantly driving radical change throughout an organization is very costly. It makes it impossible to become proficient in new ways before they change. A constant wave of disconnected organizational changes detracts from focusing on doing better in areas that matters. A company is a social organism; it works on human time.

Southwest Airlines became a company to reckon with by sticking to its core principles centered on customer service and operational efficiency. Amazon's relentless focus on what customers want—better prices, faster delivery, and more options—has made it hugely successful. It did not allow itself to get stuck. It adheres to its core beliefs, and is willing to turn away from stray paths. Adobe used to run an annual planning cycle where the main focus would change every year. It would take the then ten-thousand-person company six months to define, plan, share, and staff according to the new direction. It was almost impossible to reach any meaningful goal in the six months before the plan would change. Apple, before the turnaround, focused on customers' needs a little too much. As a result, it ended up with more than ten variations of the personal computer, which led to total customer confusion. After the turnaround, it took almost five years before the new direction was successful. But during those five years, there was a clear focus on simplicity and customer value. The iMac and iPod were the outcome of such laser focus.

What makes a company successful in the long run is the adherence to an end goal, or a vision, that does not change frequently. This vision must be centered on elements that can weather time. It should not be focused on a particular technology or product, but rather, on the value these solutions provide while reaching for the end goal, the vision. At the same time, the company must react to changing demands, but not at the cost of sacrificing the end goal, the vision. So balancing flexibility and focus is what you do.

The above stories make the point that the right operational model can get you closer to your goals, to your vision. A model is about agreeing on how to do things. The better aligned it is to your goals, the faster you can reach them. In order to achieve your goals, you create a vision; you set directions. A vision is the cornerstone of an operational model. Everything else is built around it. Anything anyone does should be in support of this vision. How do you make that happen? Not by e-mailing goals and vision, but by building an operational model that makes it easy to spend time on making the vision a reality. Every day, everyone should embody the model, the vision. The closer adherence to the model, the faster you move toward your vision so you can realize the company's true purpose.

How Versus What

Solving technical challenges by engineering a solution is the fun part. That is what engineers do best. This is what our reward systems are built around. It is from these areas that most managers and leaders emerge. They have been able to produce success by showing tangible results. Often, company results come from excellence in a smaller part of the organization. A few groups are doing really well because they are focused. This then can easily become the way a leader thinks about success. Enable some small teams to do well. In this frame of mind it is very easy to set aside the larger organization's potential. Leaders have a choice: short-term gain focused on a few heroes versus long-term growth where the whole company is engaged in common goals.

Unfortunately, not many leaders emerge from enabling a larger organization working within a fine-tuned methodology. Rarely do you see a leader being promoted and rewarded for focusing on building lasting organizational performance ("lasting" meaning many years). But you do see leaders being promoted for fixing a problem or delivering a fantastic product, regardless of impact on the organization and partners.

This can lead to a company with strong leaders who know how to build products but are unable to work together. Each one of the strong leaders knows how to manage his or her own group by making decisions for them as needed. This behavior is often reinforced by creating business units, or other independent groups, each with individual profit goals. This may work if the units are truly independent and can cover the cost of duplication of common areas, such as internal tools and marketing. But for the most part, a company is a company because it wants to leverage its know-how as much as possible. If you have invested and gained industry recognition for your customer support, you want every part of the company to benefit. You don't want one group that feels "special" establishing its own way of providing support. This can be said for many functions within a company. You want to adopt best practices across the company; therefore, you need your leaders to work together in meaningful ways.

It is easier to build an operational model for smaller teams compared with larger groups. I have noticed significant differences between small teams, groups of two hundred to three hundred, divisions of a thousand to fifteen hundred, and many thousands. What works well for one does not always work well for another. When a leader moves among the different size organizations, he or she often underestimates the effort and insight it takes to adjust his or her managerial approach.

The inevitable result: constant chaos. Leaders with big ideas, who lack experience in implementing them across larger organizations. In no time, you have frustrated managers, wandering teams, the creation of working groups or steering committees, and top-down short-lived initiatives. This is a perfect environment for heroes: smart, independent people who can deliver a solution, a product. But at a high cost. You may get something done, but the majority of the organization, the horsepower of the company, is not engaged. Instead, they are classified as B players, as people who just need to show up to make the company work. And that is just what you get: B players.

A Versus B

Who are the B players? Are they people who will never find a place where they can make a difference, or are they people who are simply not capable and never will be?

Clearly, we can all get better at what we are doing. We cannot all climb Mount Everest. But for sure, we can all contribute in some way. When faced with deadlines or when tired, we tend to be less tolerant of people who are not contributing at the level we expect. And the temptation is to then start placing people into performance buckets.

Every Role Matters

For many years, I coached my children playing recreational soccer. Every fall, I would show up and meet a group of children who had been assigned to the team. A few players really knew the sport. Most could move around and kick the ball on occasion. Many of them had never played before. Some of them did not even want to be there. But as it would give parents a few hours of free time, soccer was a popular sport.

Volunteers ran the league. They had a good program, or an operational model, to manage the many teams and about fifteen hundred young players. As a coach I had to attend classes about motivating young soccer players. Two coaches, brothers from the UK, normally led the lessons. Their message made me change my coaching style, and improve my leadership approach.

The core of their message was that every player will get better if they participate. It is impossible for someone not to improve if they spend four to five hours per week for twelve weeks on a field kicking a soccer ball. So the coach's role is to allow them to touch the ball and play as much as possible. How that is done is less important. As long as the players are motivated and participating, they will improve.

A coach is also responsible for making sure that every player has fun. A coach cannot only focus on the best players. It is easy to do, as they can follow the drills. A coach must make sure that little Johnny, who is on the sideline crying because someone stepped on his foot, gets back in the game. Even if he refuses to play, a coach cannot ignore him. Johnny is on the team. It is the coach's responsibility to bring him back in the game. If needed, the coach must take the time to explore how to remove Johnny's concerns. There is no way out for the coach. The league's purpose is to provide young children the rewarding experience of a team sport, such as soccer. The measure of success for a coach is to make sure every player has fun and improves.

So it is with an organization. A leader must care for everyone in the organization. A leader must stop and pause to make sure that every person is motivated and can contribute at his or her level. And that is how you tap into the potential of the whole organization. You get everyone to participate. Forget the A versus B. In the alphabet, every letter has its place.

It is a company effort to make an operational model successful. Just like preparing a plane for flight, everyone has a role. And everyone with a role gets to participate. An operational model should tap into everyone's potential.

Direction is a vision built into an operational model to focus energy of the whole organization toward whatever you want your company to become.

2

Where Do You Start?

Before you start making changes, or building a new operational model, it is always best to look at what you already have. What is working, and what is not? What is documented, and what is not? Capture it all. Try to understand it. Make it a full-time effort for a while. What is seen from one angle in the organization is only a sliver of the whole. You have to move around, seek input, and be open to criticism. This is not an exercise to validate you or anyone else in the company. This is a time of honesty, looking in the mirror, and capturing the real company, not the glossy version.

Listen

Everywhere, there are people with an opinion. Your role is to capture, organize, and make sense of it. Remember to include customers, employees, partners, and stakeholders. Each group is unique and may require a different approach. Depending on your relationships with these groups, some will offer up their suggestions easier than others.

You should let your company and situation guide your questions. Your situation will be unique. But in regards to the operational model, here are some questions to consider when asking the various groups.

- How do we create value or make an impact?
- How do we measure success?
- Are the right people working on the right things?
- Do we bring the right people together at the right time to address new problems and opportunities?
- Are new ideas heard and implemented?
- Why are some activities centralized and others distributed?
- Do we work well together?
- Can we make and implement important decisions faster than the competition?
- Is it clear how important decisions are made?

A good way of getting feedback is to do simple surveys of ten to fifteen questions. They could be organized around products, industry trends, or how employees can influence their immediate groups in order to move the company forward. Whatever you select, try to make them timeless. By standardizing the questions, you can use them again at a later time. This can then become a data point for measuring your ability to improve the operational model. I would caution about using surveys too often; my experience is once per quarter is what most people can tolerate.

A survey is a signal saying you care and will take drastic measures to fix things. If this is not what you had in mind, then do not use surveys. Employees will see through you. We have all completed surveys that result in nothing. If you cannot deliver something very visible as a result of the survey, don't use them. The number-one problem with surveys at work is that employees have low confidence in them. They believe that owners of the survey (i.e., management) are unable to use the survey results to make meaningful change. If using employee surveys, make them simple, short, and not too frequent, and get the unfiltered results back to employees quickly. Don't send them to an outside party that gives you the interpreted results back three months later.

Another way to gain insight into an organization is to get people together in small groups. Ask questions about their challenges, ideas, or complaints. It can be done fairly quickly. In a few hours, you can collect a wide range of information about your company.

One effective way of obtaining clarity in the face of chaos is to get people together in groups of fifteen to twenty. Have a neutral facilitator run a fact-finding session on what works well and what doesn't. Have the facilitator take the group through organizing the findings into like items. Then look for cause and effect. If it all goes well, you end up with a fishbone diagram, a picture of what issues lead to other issues. In this way, you can better understand causes versus symptoms. In the sample below you should start looking into A and C as drivers for issues B, D and E.

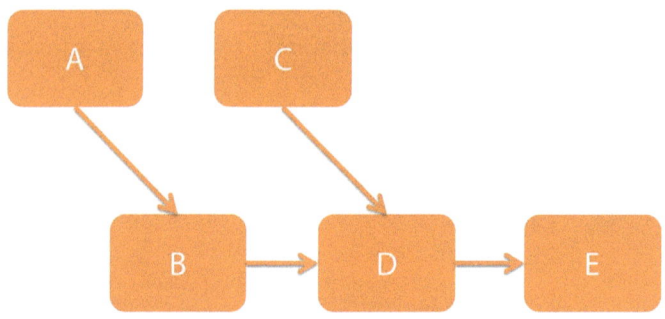

Lastly, it might be worth sitting down with people individually and dive into their world. This works well, but it takes more time to collect, assemble, analyze, and comprehend the findings.

In the end, it really does not matter how you collect the data. Problems and opportunities in a company are not hidden. There is a collective understanding of how everything works. We are, after all, social beings. We have a built-in need for sharing. We enjoy commiserating misfortunes and celebrating successes. We have friends and colleagues at work in whom we confide. Even our managers share information that might be labeled restricted.

One of the misnomers at work is "need-to-know." In other words, keep information limited to a smaller set of employees. This works fine in areas where it is a core part of how they operate. For example, insider information such as sales and revenue figures are more easily contained because there are legal consequences for sharing them. The systems and tools are set up to keep this information restricted. In meetings, people are aware of what to share and what not to share. The legal community is built upon keeping information restricted. It is a totally different matter when it comes to layoffs, reorganizations, or people behaving badly. There are normally limited or no legal consequences for sharing this with fellow employees. Keeping this type of information contained is seen as an arbitrary wish from someone in the company, and often ignored,

There are no secrets at work. I spent more than a decade in one of the most secretive public high-tech companies in the world. I was always amazed at how quickly I was able to learn about "top-secret" decisions, usually within twenty-four hours of them being made. I did not have to try. People just love to share. Yes, there are exceptions. Yes, sometimes you find yourself on the outside. But not when it comes to prevalent issues. Those are easily found. All you have to do is listen; you don't even have to ask.

Learn

So what are you looking for? Anything at all. Once you have information, organize it in like items. Put them into categories that make sense for you. Don't start out with predefined categories of issues, such as engineering problems, IT problems, HR issues, and so forth. Very often, issues are interconnected and span the whole company. For example, if you don't have visibility in the product pipeline, every part of the organization suffers. You can't plan for localization, sales promotions, support, patent filings, and more. In this example, you could ask the legal department to fix their late patent reviews, but this is a symptom of something else—not the root cause.

Here is a simple way of capturing the status quo. Doing it this way forces you to slow down, and prevents you from jumping to action. I have added some guiding text, but it should be replaced with your findings, analysis, and possible next steps.

#	Status Quo	Analysis	Possible Next Steps
1	Describe the situation.	What does it mean?	What to do?
2	Use neutral words.	Why is it a problem?	Do we need more info?
3	Don't blame anyone.	Is it an opportunity?	Do we have a plan?
4	Keep it short.	Is more analysis needed?	What's the next milestone?

Again, the purpose of this exercise is to gain introspection, not to show that you are wonderful. We already know that. What you are seeking is to do better. And that will only happen if you are honest, and look at everything as a springboard for improvement. It is easy to just get by. Almost any effort will suffice if that is your goal. Greatness is a long-term commitment that requires daily effort.

Reflect

You have done the collection and analysis, and outlined some next steps. This is a perfect time to step back and reflect. As with any change to an organization, it comes with a cost. The cost could be reduced productivity or lowered morale. On the other hand, the benefits should align with what you are hoping to achieve: employee satisfaction, increased sales, better products, and happier customers. The larger the organization, and the larger the change, the higher the cost of change. But the results are not always proportionate. Meaning, a big investment in a large organization may not lead to better products or increased employee satisfaction. Therefore, before making changes, take a close look at the cost versus projected benefits. Is the difference worth the price? Also, remember the more initiatives you have, the less chance of success for any one of them.

An organization has an upper limit for digesting change. It is important to understand what that limit is. My experience is that an organization can successfully accept, at most, two major changes and a handful of smaller ones at any given time. Any more, and you have confusion. It becomes difficult to identify what is important because the more initiatives you have, the less time you have to respond to each one of them. As a result, people tune out and disperse into their own teams to find sanctuary to ride out the storm.

One approach to limiting the number of changes impacting any one group is to make focused changes. Say you have one large initiative that spans the company. Then, follow that up with one or two initiatives tailored to each group. You may end with a total of ten initiatives, but no group has to digest more than three.

Leverage

Transforming a large organization with many groups is a high mountain to climb. There are many ways up. Here is an approach I have used often over the years. I started using it after a lengthy international flight where I was exchanging stories with a vice president of manufacturing and operations at a major multinational company. He was responsible for the productivity of more than one hundred sites across the world. He was very aware that he had a limited amount of time to spend with each site. Regardless, he was responsible for making every site successful. Every site had to meet its goals.

His approach was to identify three categories of sites: the top-performing three sites, the middle, and the bottom-performing three sites. He would work with the bottom three to encourage them to move toward an acceptable level. He would give them a timeline. If they made it before time ran out, then everything was well. If not, he would take more drastic measures. In either case, they were moved out of the bottom three one way or another. At the same time he would work with the top performers. What were they doing that he could learn from? He would encourage them to do better. He would also impose upon them the responsibility for sharing their methods with as many other sites as possible. He would continue working with them until another site would break into the top three and then rebalance the top performer list.

So what was the outcome? Over time, the performance of every site improved. Not only the best and the worst, but also every site in the middle. He was able to encourage more than a hundred sites to do better by working with only six sites at any given time. I was impressed.

Does It Matter?

We are all problem solvers. Any problem raised by an employee, at every level in the organization, should be addressed. A problem is raised by someone because of something they would like to change. Regardless of its importance or impact, they want it fixed. If you support this approach for an extended period, you end up with a large number of efforts that are not coordinated and compete for time. This generally leads to lack of success. Success is reached because you focus, and are willing to stay with it until you get there. Solving too many problems at once leads to failure.

One way of thinking about a problem is to take a look at the particular area and ask yourself how you are doing in relation to other groups or companies. For example, say one challenge was too many e-mails. This is a common problem. Now ask yourself: Is this better or worse than in other groups? If it is about the same, then why do anything? Why would you spend time addressing this issue if everybody in the industry has the same challenge? Will solving it make your organization better in some way? Will it lead to better products? Will it lead to improved productivity?

Now, if your answer is that your organization is doing better than others, then consider doing nothing, even if somebody is complaining. They may not have done a comparison or may be unable to manage large volumes of e-mails. Instead of imposing a company-wide initiative, consider helping the one person who complained. The main reason for taking action in this case is if you are slipping from being in a lead position, to the middle of the pack. And, maintaining the lead is critical.

On the other hand, if your organization or company is doing much worse than others, you may want to consider taking action. But before doing anything, ask yourself if this problem truly matters. Will the time and money you put into addressing this lead to an outcome that you really want? In comparison to everything else going on, does this rise toward the top? If yes, then take action. If not, drop it. Instead, focus on what really matters and that will bring you closer to your goals. Do not be tempted to take every side road, thinking the journey will be shorter. There are simply too many side roads. When a new problem or opportunity arises, start by asking yourself two questions. They are:

- How well am I doing?
- Does it matter?

In the next graph, I placed the "does it matter" question on the vertical axis, and the "how well am I doing" on the horizontal axis. I then have six categories. Only a few of them warrant actions and investment of additional time or money.

Should I Invest More Time or Money?		
It Matters	Yes, if…	Rarely	Yes, if…
It Does Not	No!	No!	No!
	Behind	Performing	Leading

Place every problem or opportunity that requires extra effort into the graph. If it doesn't matter, drop it! Do not be tempted to spend time just because you can, or because someone is complaining. It may not help you reach success. If it does matter, consider investing if you are behind or leading. If you are ahead and want to stay there, you may want to continue investing. If you are behind and it is critical to catch up, then consider investing there as well. If you are doing as well as anybody else, leave it alone. Why? Because things are working. Your own assessment was that things are OK. Look elsewhere to further your vision. Too often, we are tempted to turn something OK into perfect. Getting to perfect requires the last ninety percent of the total effort. It is very expensive to get there. Do you really need to do so? The one exception for investing more in an OK area is if it is the number-one problem in your group—the issue that will make or break it. And the only way of implementing your vision is to be ahead of everyone else in this area. If that is the case, then invest.

Now, ask yourself two more questions:

- Am I willing to live the change?
- Can I measure success?

Unless you are willing to drive the change and operate as if the outcome is inevitable, then you cannot change an organization. We are human beings. We do not follow a lost cause, or someone lost in the woods. It may look like we do, but that is only on the surface. A critical survival skill of human kind is to follow a leader, but not necessarily being committed to the cause. It is your responsibility as a leader to not allow this to happen.

When have you arrived? You don't want to continue beyond what will solve the problem. You need to know when you have arrived. Therefore, do your best describing what success looks like. It may not be a number. It may be a set of outcomes or behaviors. Once you get there, reevaluate. Do you want to set the bar higher, and therefore, continue to invest? Or do you see a better opportunity somewhere else?

It is easy to get a small group of people together and make the best plans. You can attempt to run the world from spreadsheets and presentation software. As a leader, it is simple to delegate your ideas to others. But the responsibility for success cannot be delegated. That stays. A leader is a role model. Whatever a leader embodies is what others emulate. If you delegate the responsibility for success and then forget about it, very little will happen.

You may want some things really, really badly. But desire is not enough to make an organization change. A leader must be up front and lead the charge. But before you start, have an approach. Build your plan around things that matter. Things that will move the whole company forward.

The extraordinary side effect of asking yourself the above four questions is that they limit the number of improvement efforts and the amount of organizational changes. It therefore makes it clear for everyone what is really important. Because of this, it is easier for everyone to focus his or her energy on those few critical things.

Now What?

Hopefully this has provided you with some guidance on how to approach your list of potential changes or improvements for your organization or company. Set this information aside for use when you create your operational model, and then decide where to invest in order to implement your vision. The next chapters will take you through how to build an operational model that will allow you to make your vision come to life.

Start by scanning the organization for issues and challenges, analyze the findings, and step back and reflect.

3

The Operational Model

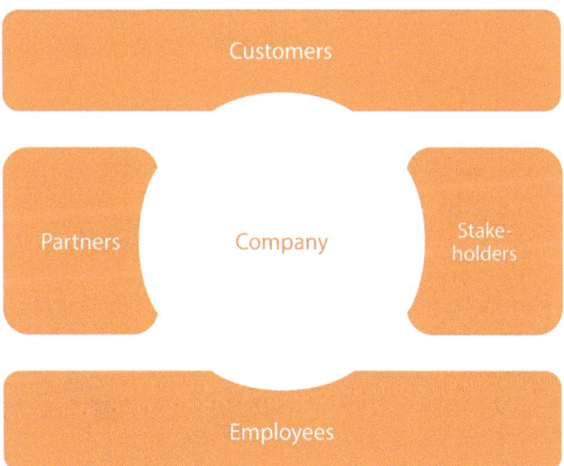

Regardless of the name and the many variations a company can have, it comes to life in the midst of employees, owners, stakeholders, customers, and partners. A company exists as a result of the interactions among these groups. It functions because every group has accepted and understood the concept behind being a company.

Customers pay the bill. They are the judge and jury. They will (correctly or incorrectly) make decisions that will make your company successful or not. A company may refer to society as a benefactor from their efforts. Many firms have stated goals of being socially responsible, being part of the community. Often a company will donate products or money to what they consider good causes. Society is not what we normally think of as a customer, but they are benefiting from the company in some way.

Stakeholders are the owners. They are the founders, the shareholders, and special interests. And to some extent, the government, which has imposed rules and regulations on companies.

Partners, such as suppliers, resellers, and other outside groups, are needed to make a company function. I cannot think of a company that is independent from partners. A consultant may need a rented office. He or she may need a computer, a phone, and access to Internet. A monk needs a place to worship; he also needs clothes and food. A guide needs transportation to take visitors to new and exciting places. An author needs an editor and proofreader. As noted earlier, we are social beings. We depend upon each other. In this book I will use the word "partners" to describe all the external groups a company depends on to operate.

Employees can be paid, or not. Regardless, they are agents of the company. They make things happen. They carry the operational model on their back. A company becomes successful when everyone has a role to play.

There might be special groups that are not listed in this model. If they are critical to your company or group, think about why that is and how you can incorporate them into your model. Sometimes you need to focus on special groups that are pivotal to making changes. Perhaps design partners are critical for your success. Maybe your customer support is outsourced and you need to make big improvements in that space. If so, just call them out and incorporate them under the "partner" umbrella.

If you run a group within a large company, the model will work just fine. You may have internal and external customers. You may have internal and external partner groups. Your stakeholders may be the senior leadership of the company. Your employees are those from your group. The approach is the same for either the whole company or a part of it. In the latter case, you are still running a "company," meaning, you have responsibility for a group that is tasked with a set of deliverables. And you, as leader, are responsible for the success of the group. If someone in your group or company does not deliver as planned, then that falls back to you.

The moment you abdicate this responsibility is the moment the operational model starts failing. You own it. You may not have designed or implemented it, but it is there. It may not be understood or documented. It may not even be managed. Regardless, it is there, and you are responsible.

Think about a birthday party of yours. If the pizzas did not arrive on time, or you ran out, it is yours to own. Yes, you can assign blame to the delivery service, but it still impacts your party. You have to fix problems that arise, or, better yet, make sure problems do not surface in the first place by implementing and operational model that is designed for success.

The Glue

The major groups of a company are customers, partners, stakeholders, and employees. These groups can be divided into subgroups as needed. The glue that binds each of these groups to the company is shown in the next graph.

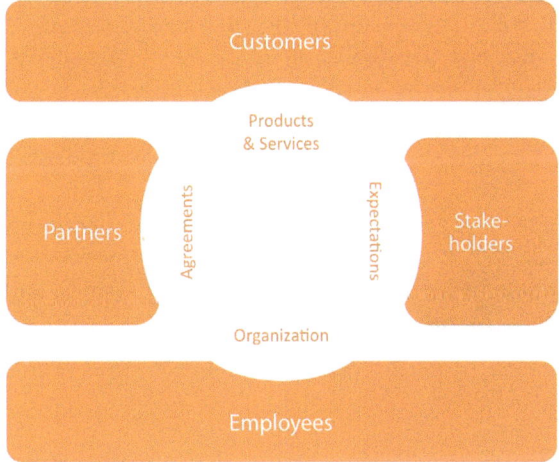

A customer's main interaction with a company is with its products and services. There are many types of companies. Some you interact with more directly when the service is provided. For others, you may only interact with the product. An airline brings you from here to there. Your interaction with the company is short. Your impression of the company is the sum of the travel experience, or, in other words, the service they provided you. If you buy an iPhone, it is with you for a longer time. You probably bought it from an Apple store or from the company website. When you think of Apple, you think about your iPhone. We associate a company with the value they bring us through their products and services.

Partners fill the gaps—whatever a company cannot achieve on its own, they are there to help. What governs the relationship with partners is all the agreements put in place. By definition, partners are not employees, and therefore, cannot be managed in a similar way. Although, it is not uncommon to think of partners as an extension of the organization. But it's best to let partners be partners. Let them manage themselves. Be clear on what you expect, the outcomes, and what the rewards are. Manage that part. Manage the agreements.

The organizational structure is what very often becomes the image of a company. We list the company name. Then there is a CEO, a CFO, a vice president, several groups, a leader, a manager, and number of individual contributors. They all have lines attached to their names. This is what we as a society often think of as the company: a tree structure with nodes and directional connections. This structure implies information flow, decision-making, salary, and status. It organizes us in a way that is very familiar and has been working since the dawn of humankind. But in the end, employees are organized to define, develop, deliver, and support products and services.

Stakeholders have expectations of the company. They do not want to manage the company or group directly, but they monitor and influence the activities and outcomes. They want the company to meet its goal and avoid failure. They want the company to do well.

The Fuel

What makes all this work is the operational model. It is the invisible, but also tangible force. It is what distinguishes greatness from simply hanging on. It is like a black hole of a solar system: you do not see it but everything around it is influenced by it. The black hole determines the movements of all objects in the solar system. You cannot avoid it. And the same is true for the operational model.

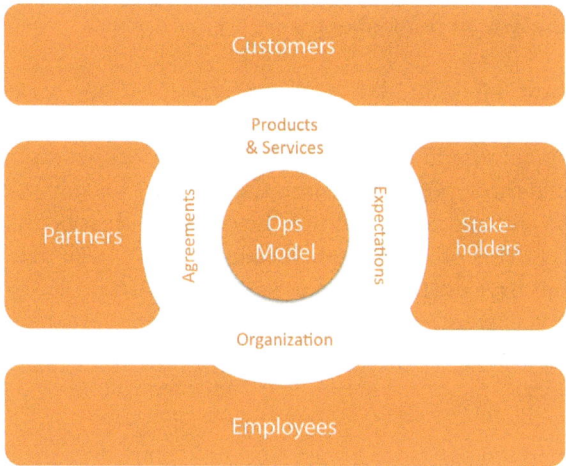

So what happens in the operational model? In short, everything. The main reason for focusing on the model is that it can be managed. It can be tuned for what you think of as success. It does not mean you have to manage everything. In fact, you should strive to manage only the factors that will transform the company to what you want it to become.

For example, we often think that people must be told what to do in much detail. So we may spend a lot of time and money based upon that assumption. Have you ever purchased a chair from IKEA? It comes in a box with detailed assembly instructions. Without them you are lost. If you purchase an elegant chair from an auction house, it is probably already assembled. You are not looking for instructions, but rather, a great location for the chair. In this obvious example, we can quickly assess when assembly instructions are needed.

When running a company, it is not that easy to figure what type of organizational instructions to provide and when to provide them. Often we end up with an overwhelming number of roles, responsibilities, and tasks. Which ones are needed? Which ones are not?

In a company, it is typical to run into problems along the way that require a large amount of people to put in extra efforts to overcome a looming crisis. Aside from being costly, it also detracts from getting everything else done. If this repeats too often, the company may lose sight of its vision. Some level of calm is needed to aim for and reach important goals. The idea behind an operational model is to prepare for what is ahead—to allow you to think about what is coming next.

Often, these are referred to as what-if scenarios. The better description of these possible events you can create, the better you can design your model. Any model should assume that crisis will occur without warning. Therefore, build those possibilities into the model. Build a model that can address a crisis without shutting down the company. Just because someone has determined that a problem is important does not mean that the best thing to do is to have everyone step in to solve it. Instead, assign the problem to an owner as outlined by the operation model, and step back. Let the model resolve the problem as you have designed it. Don't make every issue a special case, thereby undermining your own vision.

At Apple in the hardware group, we would sometimes be informed when partners had to stop production because of quality problems on the manufacturing line. It is very expensive to have a whole factory sit idle. If it lasts a long time, it also impact sales, as there will not be products to sell. Sometimes teams at the site would replace the failed part with another type, and restart the line. But if that new part was not qualified to work with the computer or if it had a long delivery lead time, it would spell disaster. Other times, the firmware or software was updated by a partner that temporarily resolved the issue. In critical cases the Apple development teams would eventually stop their current work to address the growing crisis. After many difficult episodes, where factories were sitting idle, and with an increasing product return rate from unhappy customers, something had to be done.

So we implemented *line-down escalation.* A factory could stop manufacturing at any time to fix a problem, but they could not implement a solution outside the given instructions. If they could not resume production within twenty-four hours, they had to escalate to one vice president, who had a small team designated to manage these issues. Within four hours of escalation, a resolution team with all impacted parties was assembled. A plan for resolving the problem was sent out to all partners and internal teams. Daily updates followed until the problem was solved and the manufacturing line was back up and running. This became an important element of the operational model. It removed confusion and enabled a small, focused team to resolve the problem. What used to take weeks and negatively impacted product quality was, with this new approach, resolved within hours or days and improved product quality.

An operational model has three core parts that govern the interactions of the four major groups: customers, stakeholders, employees, and partners. One can argue that there are many more parts, and that would be correct. But it is sufficient to think about these three key parts. Why? Because it works. Too many things to manage creates confusion and will slow you down. The more you have to manage, the less time you have to make them work well. The three core parts are:

- **Purpose:** Why does the company exist? What makes it special? Does it have a set of core beliefs that guides its behaviors? Why are you doing the things you are doing? How do you measure success?

- **Roles and Responsibilities:** What is needed to support the company's purpose? In these roles, what is expected? Who are the decision makers? How are decisions made?

- **Methodologies and Tools:** How is the company going to make its purpose come alive? What are the steps needed to show results? What tools do you need to support your approach in running the company?

PRM

PRM is shorthand for **P**urpose, **R**oles and Responsibilities, and **M**ethodologies and Tools. PRM is the core of the model. The purpose drives the *why* behind everything that is being done. *Who* and *what* are identified by roles and responsibilities. And the *how*, *when*, and *where* are captured in methodologies and tools.

The first PRM challenge is to capture it and make sense of it. There are many ways of displaying it. But start simple. Start in the middle and build out. Every group and team will have their own view of the world, but they all need to link back to the company operational model in some way. In some cases you may have one operational model at the highest level of the company and different ones in within business units. How deep you want to go into each function will depend upon where you are today and where you want to be in the future. In other words, the more change you expect, the more insight you should have about the status quo.

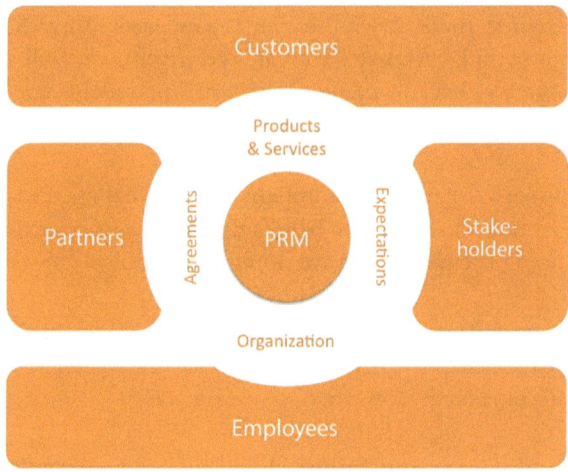

It is critical to capture how important decisions are made. Who is making them and what input is used? Quality decision-making will allow the organization to work better. Therefore, it is important to identify them in your model.

If you can, make the operational model visual. Use diagrams that show how everything connects and how value is created for your customers. Scan the Internet for ideas on what could work for your group or company. Once you have a good view of your model, invite groups to add details for their areas. Make it transparent. Invite comments and feedback. Shine lights on duplications and things that may not be aligned.

Location

Everyone in a company is looking for clarity and ways to make his or her job simpler. PRM makes that happen. Therefore, invest in it. When the blueprints for how to run the company are made available to everyone, the results are amazing.

I am not advocating that the governance of an operational model be placed into a central group. But it needs to live somewhere. And to keep it alive, someone needs to care for it.

Normally, larger organizations have areas of core expertise that are just too expensive to duplicate in every group. For example, lawyers. You keep that expertise in central groups so you have a consistent approach to patent review, signing legal documents, defending the company from lawsuits, and so forth. The same can be said for payroll. You keep that function in one group because you only need one way to pay employees. And if distributed and different approaches are used, it can create chaos and have a large negative impact.

When you talk about areas such as development tools, process standardization, program management, user interface design, and so forth, the lines are less clear. You can argue from either side. I am neutral. Do what makes sense. You have to agree upon how each group or team in the company is expected to behave, and that will require someone to do work. How this is done depends upon your preference. You may want to keep some things central, while expecting each group to do some things on their own.

Either way, keeping what matters, such as an operational model, front and center requires time and effort. It does not come for free. Expect to pay for what you get. If this is nobody's job, you get less. If it is your job, you get more. If you get help, you get even more done.

An operational model connects customers to products and services, stakeholders to expectations, employees to the organization, and partners to agreements. A company is driven by its purpose, roles and responsibilities, and methodologies and tools.

4

Setting Directions

How do you improve an operational model and outline a new path? How do you set a direction toward the desired future state of your company? This has been done before. It is done every day. The easiest and perhaps most prevalent approach is to allow a leader or manager to direct traffic. The leader makes all the rules, all the decisions, all the time. If anyone has a question, they know where to go. In this world, everything is easy. There is one boss; it is clear what success and failure look like. If you don't know, just ask. This is an approach that can work in smaller teams, but at a cost.

It can also work in larger groups, but at a higher cost. Constantly chasing down decisions or clamoring for time with the decision maker is a hindrance to productivity. And worse, if decisions are inconsistent and change frequently, you have chaos. Worst of all, this is an approach that does not take advantage of available skill and talent.

So a better approach is to engage your team. Share your goals. Nothing works better than gaining a common understanding of the challenges before creating an improvement plan.

Make A List

It is now time to bring out what you already know and recently learned about your company. Do your best to take your understanding of the company and fit it into the below categories. You will need this insight so you can move toward what you want your future model to look like. The categories are:

- Customers and their usage of products and services
- Stakeholders and their expectations
- Employees and the organization
- Partners and the agreements

In addition, you should include the core of the operational model:

- Purpose
- Roles and responsibilities
- Methodologies and tools

Take these seven categories and place them into a table. Write down what is taking place today. Write down what you have learned from looking across the organization, as outlined in chapter two. In addition, capture what you really want your company to become. You should fit it all on one page. One page? Yes, one page. This makes it possible to think about the model more clearly. Looking at it all on one page allows your memory to springboard into the depths of the model and its parts. Because you already spent time diving into the issues, you understand what this page signifies. Therefore, you don't need to write a book about it. If needed, you can later expand the scope to include more levels of the company, but the top level should be defined and captured first.

Complete the table on the next page with the specifics of your own company or group. Focus on the critical functions, the larger groups, and the top strategic and tactical decisions. Capture where the value is created. You may want to fill this in during a meeting with your team. Sometimes it works better to structure a series of meetings that leads up to completing this one-pager. The one-pager is the foundation for the future state of your group or company.

Area	Today	Future
Customers: Products and Services	Describe what you have today. List customer groups and products or types of products.	What are the changes you want at some point in the future? New markets? New product lines? New customers? More frequent delivery?
Stakeholders: Expectations	What do they value, what is important for them? Growth? Revenue? Societal contributions?	Do you need to make changes for stakeholders? What is your promise to them?
Employees: Organization	How are the employees organized? What is unique about them as compared to other companies?	Is there a need to change anything to meet new demands? How can you avoid constant reorganizations?
Partners: Agreements	Who are your business partners today? Why do you have them? How are the relationships with them?	Do you see them taking on more responsibilities, becoming an equal partner? What is your promise to them?
Purpose	Why are you doing what you are doing?	What do you want the future to become? Why does the company exist?
Roles and Responsibilities	Who is responsible for what? Are there overlaps? Gaps? Who makes critical decisions?	Do you need new skills? Do you need new roles? What is kept at central groups?
Methods and Tools	How are things getting done today? What is your current tool set? Are there gaps?	Are there better ways? Can a new delivery model reduce time to value? What should be managed? What should not?

Your Vision

At this point you have captured where the company is and where you want it to be. Next is the formulation of your vision. What makes a vision of the future possible is a common understanding. And as a leader, it is your responsibility to foster enough dialogue to make a painting (or vision) of the future come alive. The next graph contrasts the current and future company. This is the basis for formulating your vision.

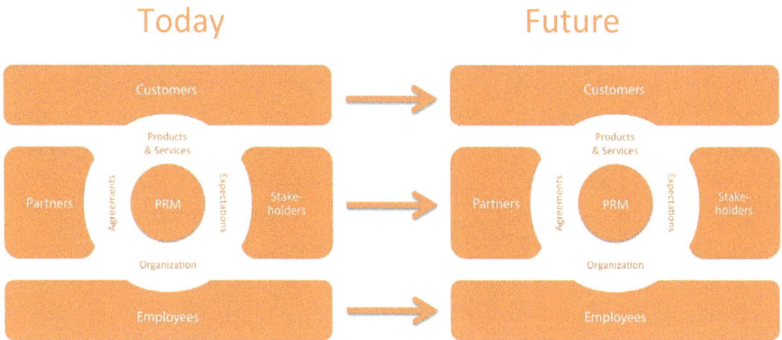

The arrows between today and the future are the gaps. It is what is missing in order for the company to realize its vision. It is what needs to be done. It is the mountain to climb. You as a leader must include the gaps when painting the vision. You must ensure that everyone understands what is expected and what it will take to be successful.

It Takes PI

Have you ever sent an e-mail to a group of your friends with directions to a party? Have they ever responded because something was not clear in your e-mail, or they brought something up that you were not aware of? Are you assuming every e-mail you send will be read and instructions followed without any questions? It is an easy trap to fall into. In a company, we should rightly assume that we are all professionals and can easily read and follow instructions. However, that is not enough when communicating a new direction.

When setting company directions what you really want is lasting change, not just a handful of e-mails followed by informational meetings. Lasting change takes place when the whole company buys into and lives the change. My manager once told me that every major company initiative has a half-life of about eighteen to twenty-four months. We have all seen them. They have many names and goals. But what they have in common is that they try to implement something new in a company, such as total quality management, cascading objectives, voice of the customer, and so forth. Very often these are inspired by a trend in the industry, meaning many other companies are doing something very similar. In some cases they are required by state or federal agencies in order to do business with them.

None of the initiatives were implemented to just create work; they had a purpose. They may not all have been timely and relevant, or addressed the most important issue to solve at the time. In many cases they were probably prescriptive, following a step-by-step approach that everyone had to adhere to. And that is why they often fail, because there is not enough flexibility to incorporate a particular initiative into everything else that a company or group must also focus their efforts on. So when you describe a company initiative, you must clearly define its purpose and criteria for success. What is in between should be flexible. A group must be given time and space to make the solution their own. We all love a challenge, something that can inspire us to be creative and allow us to come up with new ways of solving a problem. If a new initiative is seen as a list of to-do items with little room for adding value, most people lose interest. So in short, select your initiatives with the goal of creating lasting value that will make a difference, but be flexible with the implementation details.

Back to your e-mail. You sent it out, everyone attended your party, but you underestimated the amount of food required. Many people left hungry. It can happen. So it is with an organization. You cannot predict what is going to happen when leading the organization into a new space. What is certain is that it will not perform well after having tried the new approach once or even twice. My experience is that everything takes PI. After three tries the organization gets it. They can do it well. Anything before that is practice.

When I first started working at Apple, we had a really hard time completing Mac OS version 7. It took a long time. Every ship date kept getting pushed back. It was eventually *declared* it was time to ship. Once it left the building, we started working on 7.1, a release to fix everything we did not have time get done in the prior release. Shipping an operating system requires many different types of software coming together on the same timeline. There are a large number of groups and people to coordinate, both from development and supporting groups, such as localization, documentation, support, marketing, and sales. In order to manage this type of project, you need a model. So we put one in place.

We decided that we needed to manage the overall effort with a few people in charge to make the main decisions, then communicate them to everyone and let the development teams respond. On the core project team was an engineering manager, a product manager, a program manager, an architect, an international lead, and a few other representatives. This team met frequently to review progress and make decisions. They held extended team meetings to ensure communication was distributed to all team members. They would also put in place review groups for bugs (defects), features, user interface, and other issues. They would then show the organization what was expected in each of these areas. For example, if a bug was not written in a way that would allow a team to understand how to efficiently reproduce it, then it was sent back to the originator. The message was to report bugs with actionable information. This was—and probably is—a very typical way of managing a larger project. The important part of this team was that it stayed together for a number of releases. Some changes in roles took place, but the overall practices were maintained.

How many releases did it take before we could deliver in a predictable way with minimal noise and surprises? The answer is three, meaning, the fourth release was done exceptionally well. It was managed by a team that knew what would come next. They were able to learn what to look for and address problems long before they had the opportunity to grow into a crisis. As a result, the time it took to do many of the coordinating activities went down, because there were fewer exceptions. And that is a well-run project.

Fast-forward a few years and I was at Adobe, part of delivering our suite of products (a collection of products you can purchase as a bundle). What struck me when joining project meetings was the total absence of a common understanding of what would happen next during a development cycle. The people on the project teams were not the same from release to release. The definition of what it meant to be part of a suite shifted over time. The way the suite was managed changed as well, so there was no way of building a performing team. However, later when a core team was put in place, it started to improve. Utilizing similar approaches as at Apple, the delivery of suites became predictable. It may not have solved all the company's challenges, but the project was performing well. Then it changed. A new group took the lead in delivering Adobe products via the Internet, instead of shipping CDs. And the whole learning process started again. It is possible to regress when the value of organizational experience is placed behind technical expertise.

As you get closer to selecting your initiatives, you should plan to make them last long enough so that they can be successful. Allow time for adjustments and improvements.

But...

It is not enough to paint a picture of the future. It is important to know why you are going there. But success lies in the how. Getting there is a journey of a thousand steps. Every one of them matters. One small misstep could be the difference between success and failure. The challenge is which one? You don't know that answer. Therefore, it is critical to make the assumption that everything in your model is important and needs consideration. It does not mean that you personally need to spend time on everything. It means if something needs to be done, it should be done the best possible way, with the best intentions, and with the assumption that it could make or break the company. If you don't take this approach, then success is a lottery. Therefore, take control. Make success a choice—not a probability.

At the same time, be ready to set it all aside. A journey of a thousand steps does not go in a straight line. It turns. It twists. It may revisit the same place twice. You may spend extraordinary time and money getting nowhere. You may have to abandon everything you brought with you on the journey because the weather or circumstances changed. What you first thought was important may no longer be. What you assumed before the very first step no longer holds true. When that happens, at that moment of realization that your world has changed, lift your head. Do not look back in agony. You are now one step closer to success. You embrace the next step as being the most important on the journey. Why? Why not? You have already decided to go on a journey. Why do you want to wallow in the sorrow of the past? Why do you want to spend energy on what was, when you can make the future come closer? You create success; it doesn't come without your determination of getting to a better future.

A Painting

Vision, mission, purpose, strategy, goals, initiatives, metrics, and success are all important for a company to have and live by. However, it can become overwhelming to keep all these terms up to date and communicate them across a larger organization. So if you have a choice, keep it simple. Pick words that fit your company.

I prefer to avoid the phrase *picture of the future*, as it implies clarity. The future is not always that clear. There are many things in this world that will want to have a say on what that picture will look like. Instead, a *painting of the future* is more reminiscent of someone having spent time and effort capturing and interpreting their understanding of the future. And at the same time, it sends the message that this may not be fully accurate, that there is some room for adjustments. So paint the future. In the next chapter, we will take that painting and turn it into a blueprint for how to change the organization.

Set a direction by making an inspiring painting of the future and contrasting it with the present picture.

5

Managing Directions

What makes an organization change and behave differently? Every company is different and has a unique culture. There are many differences across industries. We all bring distinctive strengths and have diverse cultural backgrounds. But there are also many commonalities across industries. I strongly believe that what unites us are stronger than any of our differences. There are best practices for organizational changes and many books on this topic. Here are my guiding principles for leading change that I have validated across many high-tech organizations:

- Describe the here and now
- Create a painting of the future
- Name things that will change and when
- Provide a yardstick for measuring success
- Assign an owner
- Create a stage

We've already covered the here and now and the painting of the future in the previous chapters. The painting is typically done by visionaries—senior leaders of the company or group. However, anyone can do it. Any group can create its own painting. The most common failure I have seen is that the same group that did the painting moves on to defining the details of how to implement the changes. It is here that they should bring in people who have done this before, and who will make driving change their full-time job. Very often the initiatives, the things that drive change, are copied from another company or industry. That is OK, but they must first be adjusted to fit your particular situation.

Select The What And When

The next step is to carefully select a handful of initiatives that will have the biggest impact. You don't necessarily need to implement large efforts or make large announcements. It is very tempting because you get immediate visibility and perhaps admiration for resolving a problem or defining a better way. Instead, take your time and keep the end goal in mind. Very often, a collection of small things makes a bigger impact.

Set a timeline, but don't make it too tight. You can't make an organization change overnight. You may see some swift improvements, but don't stop there. Continue to invest and improve until you reach a level that will allow you to meet your goals, to realize your vision. Your competitors in the industry are hard at work trying to get there before you. Lasting change requires lasting efforts.

Show progress toward your goals. Have a multiyear plan with regular check-ins. The assumption is that the company will be around for a while and you might as well plan for the long term. This is, of course, more challenging in start-ups where there is no tomorrow unless the whole group achieves a very specific funding level or revenue target.

Define Success

Once initiatives are identified, define what success looks like. Success can be measured in many ways. It can be a description of a set of behaviors. It can be measured by numbers or by an assessment based upon a set of variables. How you do it is up to you. It is, however, important to describe what it looks like and how it will be measured. It is important to measure the group against something it can actually influence. Asking an engineering group to work smarter and support double-digit revenue growth is not a yardstick that can be applied. It is simply too far away from what they are doing. They are already working as smartly as they possibly can. Assuming they are not is an insult, or a display of mistrust. Engineers have little to do with the sales of products. They build products. They are not selling them. Select measures such as release cycles, feature impact, agility, or quality levels. Other groups may have different measures, but tailor them to their span of influence.

Assign An Owner

Allow each of the initiatives to be driven like a project. Provide regular status reports, hold review meetings, and share information widely across the company. But most important of all, assign an owner: someone who makes this a personal quest, and someone who can understand that owning it means you *are* it. If you assign ownership to more than one person, then you have many places for failure. If you assign it to one, you know where success will be driven from.

Create A Stage

So far, what I have described is very normal. But it is what makes an organization change. What eventually will tip the scale is the stage. Create a place where the owners and the teams are given an opportunity to shine (or fail). Place them in front of the group on a regular basis to talk about progress. Make as many team members as possible go on stage. There is nothing more powerful than knowing you have a large group of people staring at you. This is a principle that is universally applied for many types of situations where people are trying to make some sort of change. It is applied in support groups where you go and talk about your progress; it can be applied to reports that need to be written and presented at school or at work. The list is endless.

So create a stage. It can be virtual. It does not need to be in one room. It is more powerful when everyone is present, but many companies today are very distributed. Strive to bring people together on some frequency and place them on the stage (an "all-hands" meeting of sorts). The audience can vary. You may have a stage where the audience is the whole group. You may have another stage where the audience is the core leaderships of the company, or another part of the company. You decide. The thing to keep in mind is that it takes practice to run through a good stage performance. Not only do you need to know all your facts, you also need to know how to present them well. And most of all, you need to know your audience. Make the stage presence short and simple, with a small audience. Over time, add more people and more content to the presentations.

In addition, you may want to use newsletters, company websites, and other similar means to extend the stage. In most companies, there is an abundance of information online. Most of it is placed into an unstructured system that makes it very challenging to find. Give it some time, and most of it becomes outdated. Therefore, refer to your online stage in meetings to keep it current. Share the online stage and point people to it. Soon, it becomes a destination because you made it relevant. Enroll the organization in using the online stage to present their progress, including both successes and failures. Note: a stage cannot be a project status report on a website next to a hundred other reports.

Initiatives

Here is a simple template for listing your initiatives. The total list should not be more than one page. Having too many pages communicates a lack of focus. It says you a problem, but you are not sure how to solve it, so you're going to start a number of things, hoping something will happen. One project says, "I'm focused on one thing that is important, and everything else is not important." In order to engage the whole group or company, a handful of initiatives are normally sufficient.

Initiative	Description	Goal	Owner	Timeline
Initiative 1	Brief description	What is the desired end state? How will it be measured?	One Name	Milestones and dates
Initiative 2	Brief description	You can use numbers to measure.	One Name	Milestones and dates
Initiative 3	Brief description	A measure can be changed behavior.	One Name	Milestones and dates

Roadmap

Another way of showing the initiatives is to lay out their deliverables over time—a roadmap. Here is a simple roadmap template.

Initiative	Q1	Q2	Q3	Q3
Agile Development	Defined	Team Staffed	Training	50% Trained, Tool in Place
Milestone Reviews	Team Staffed	Project Reviews Start	Metrics in Place	100% Reviewed
Partner Engagement Model	Model in Place	Engage Partners	5 of 10 Using New Model	10 Using New Model

Sharing

Once you have your initiatives defined, you must ensure that everyone is aware of them and that they are *the changes* that will move the company forward. Everywhere you go, bring the list and refer to it whenever possible. If you don't, you are sending a message that you have moved on to the next thing, and no longer believe in the initiatives that will bring the company or group into the future. Stay on message.

Be A Gardener

A leader is like a gardener. A gardener has three responsibilities. First, preparing the soil and planting seedlings or seeds. Then comes watering and fertilizing. Lastly, the gardener removes weeds, so what was planted can grow and prosper.

A leader has the same three responsibilities. First, prepare the organization for new ideas and new goals. The leader lets people know that the status quo is not enough, and that problems exist and opportunities are all around. Then a vision is created, a destination is defined.

The leader then spends time and effort promoting the new direction. Whenever someone takes a step toward the new direction, the leader applauds, rewards, and recognizes the effort. Just like a plant, a new idea requires time to grow and prosper. So the leader must applaud every little step, every day. A plant does not grow by receiving an enormous amount of water twice per year. It grows when there is a steady supply of water. An important part of praise is to support the intent of moving in the new direction, the effort, and the desire. Focus less on the outcome. Just like a tree branch grows, you cannot predict direction and shape, but it will grow to become part of a perfect tree. Over time, the organization will do better and will become great at what it is doing. Consider using everything from a thank you to an increase in salary. It is not critical where anybody starts. It is critical to support the improvement toward something better.

Finally, a leader must remove competing ideas, efforts, or anything that is blocking the vision from prospering. If a gardener allows weeds to grow, the plant will suffer. The same happens in a company. Lack of weeding creates many organizational problems. I am not saying that these problems were created maliciously. In one way or another, they make it difficult for new ideas to grow. One typical challenge that prevents employees from moving toward something new is that their current workload is just too high. There is no time to spend on anything new. You often get into that situation where projects are driven by a schedule, with too many tasks attached. Another problem is when there already are a number of initiatives in the works. That could be a new salary compensation planning process, a new project-tracking tool, an effort to change the development processes, or a focus on moving all technologies to the cloud. The list goes on. It could also be that the organization is not set up to encourage groups to work together. They may have been given different goals, and may be measured in different ways. If any of these prevent new ideas from taking hold, then that is your weed. Your role as a leader is to remove it.

A leader is like a gardener. A gardener plants a specific seed because he or she wants to transform it into a full-grown plant. Once it is in the ground, a seed will not become something it was not meant to be. Therefore, selecting the right seed is important. Another distinction is that the gardener does not do the growing. The plant does. So it is with an organization. A leader does not do the work for the organization. The whole purpose of forming a company, an organization, is to allow it to run as defined by an operational model. Therefore, a leader must allow the organization to learn, improve, and succeed.

Give managers and teams time and space to grow. Be a gardener!

6

Optimizing Directions

Measuring success or progress toward the future state is ongoing. Managing directions is about focusing on key areas upon which you want to improve. The assumption is that as you improve, the benefits will outweigh the investment and make the company more successful. In addition to measuring success directly, you should also look at the company as a portfolio of investments. Everything you do takes time and money. Even if you are doing well in one area you should ask yourself if it is better to spend time and money in another area with better returns.

For example should you design your own circuit board or should you have a partner do it for you? If this is critical to your business and you are willing to invest to become good at it, then perhaps the answer is yes. If this is just something you only need for a few products, then perhaps you should find a partner. However, in many areas it is not obvious that you have a choice to make. This chapter will encourage you to think about your choices so you can optimize your overall investment of time and money.

But first, let's do a quick recap. A company is formed and operates in the midst of customers, stakeholders, employees, and partners. Customers see the company via products and services. Stakeholders define and monitor their expectations of the company. Employees are linked to the company with an organizational structure, while partners are managed by agreements.

What makes one company behave different from any other is the operational model, which at its core is about purpose, roles and responsibilities, and methodologies and tools. Leaders set directions, create an inspiring painting of the future, by contrasting the current and future state of each of the above parts. They manage progress toward the vision by carefully defining a set of initiatives and a measure of success. Each initiative is driven by one owner that is given a stage to demonstrate progress.

Before Optimization

Something has to occur before you arrive at the point where most of the organization is closely aligned with the company directions. It is not that people or groups are trying to go somewhere else, but rather, it is inherently difficult to organize larger groups in a way that takes full advantage of every person's ability to contribute. You may see alignment as a result of a big event, a shared management belief, an exceptional leader, critical mass, or implementing a model such as the one outlined in this book.

An example of a big event is lowered revenue or lack of funding. In these cases, leadership is forced to look at options. One is to reduce the size of the organization. Normally this results in lowered morale, confusion, and a setback in the path toward the future. We have all seen it. But nonetheless, it is perhaps the most widely used and accepted path for resolving differences between cost and revenue. Another type of big event is funding for a start-up, or a rapid revenue growth. Regardless, these types of events can act as catalysts for moving the company in lock step toward a new direction.

A shared management belief about how to manage a company can take place everywhere. What enables a shared belief to take place is respect: respect for each other as people, and for you as a leader. This fosters willingness to listen and cooperate, making it possible to set directions.

Who is an exceptional leader? We can all probably think of a few. All leaders come with pros and cons. Their methods may or may not be what you are willing to support. One the other hand, an exceptional leader can make a difference. They know how to move an organization toward a common vision.

What do I mean by critical mass? It is when many parts of the company are more or less successfully tapping into the efforts of most employees. The organization has a clear set of product priorities. It has been given room to operate by the stakeholders, and is leveraging partners to fill its own capability gaps. There is an absence of crisis. You can feel the low humming, like a powerful racing engine before acceleration. This strangely calming hum exudes confidence. You can notice it when you are inside the organization, or when talking to customers. Each group is peacefully operating under their own local model. In this situation it is easier to set an overall vision and work on joining the local models to an overall company operational model.

In summary, before you can start optimizing, the groups must operate under a well-defined model. It is very difficult to optimize chaos or an undefined system. It becomes almost impossible to make improvements when there is limited understanding of cause and effect. It is also impossible to optimize a system in which there is no understanding of the long-term goal, the vision, the direction. It is easy to make local improvements, but that is not what you are trying to do when optimizing a company. Therefore, the best time to optimize is after you have a clear understanding of your operational model and a painting of your future company.

Optimization

Optimization is making customers happy by delivering products and services they really want while minimizing overall cost, meeting stakeholders' expectations, fulfilling partner agreements, and, perhaps what matters most for an organization, making the company a place that everyone would be happy to work for.

Achieving optimization takes focus and time. But it also takes careful assessment of all the parts. Are they the right ones? Are there better ones? One of the main considerations when optimizing is to lean toward engaging as many people as possible in the right behavior versus excellence in a few smaller groups. It is far easier to make one small group do well. But that is not how you run a company. Running a company or large group requires a very different approach. It is no longer about one part; it is about the whole system. There is nothing wrong with having groups doing really well, but not if they do so at the expense of the majority of the company. You must strive to create a situation where everyone is engaged and all groups are doing really well. Unless everyone is engaged in the new direction, understand their part, and is encouraged to improve, you are wasting fuel. Your average miles per gallon is lower than what it could be. If you can engage the whole company on what matters, then you're golden.

Return on investment (ROI) is a term often used in the financial world. It is a way of comparing different investment options. The goal is, of course, to select the best one so you get a better return on your investment. When looking at ROI, there is often an inverse correlation to risk. The higher the risk—meaning the less of a chance that the outcome will be good—the better the return. A lottery ticket is kind of like this. It promises a very high return for a little money. The chances of winning are, of course, low. I mention risk because you must include this when looking at options. For example, should I develop a software program in-house or hire another company? You have more control in-house, but you may get it developed more quickly if done by an experienced company. Which has higher risk? Which has quicker return?

When assessing ROI, let's take a look at the four areas as shown in the next graph.

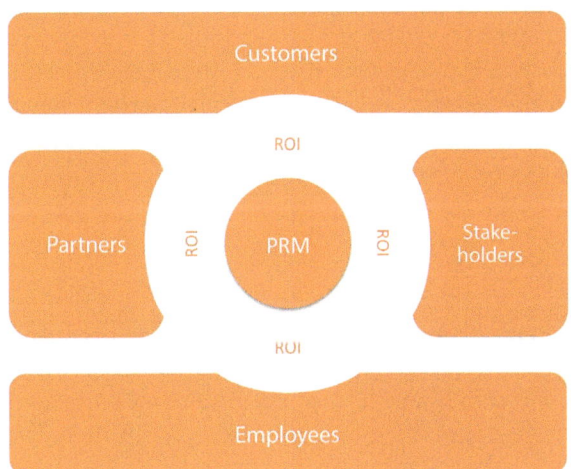

Look At The Parts

Your painting of the future has already captured your ideal company. You are now entering a phase where you're constantly reevaluating your initial assumptions. Has anything changed? Are new competitors doing better than you? Are new products entering the market? Are new technologies changing how you run software development teams? Are stakeholders expecting higher growth? Are the costs of doing business increasing in some of your locations?

Groups do not routinely do an ROI on their own parts. They prefer to improve within their own world, but may not look outside. Looking at the whole system and balancing investments requires outside encouragement, such as from company leaders. It is fully understandable that most people avoid this kind of change, and instead prefer to keep things stable as long as possible.

It is, however, the responsibility of leaders to predict what will happen next. For example, let's imagine a group that has been working together for years on a particular technology. They have achieved success and gained significant experience. In fact, they are the go-to group in the company for any issue related to this technology. Why would they want to work on something else? Let's assume that another technology in the industry is taking over and is becoming the standard. As early as possible in this shift, the group should recognize their options and set themselves up for long-term success. Unless they make plans to shift their focus at some point, they could end up being dinosaurs, working on something nobody wants. And in this position, the group will not last very long. It is therefore the leader's responsibility to consider implementing a change when appropriate to optimize chances for long-term success.

Customers

At the top level, most companies compare product lines and decide where to invest. They spend time and effort predicting future sales. Sometimes this goes well, sometimes not. At the lower levels, meaning inside a product, it is more complicated to do feature tradeoffs. Some industries are better at this than others. The automobile industry offers many options on cars. It is often these options that make up the better part of the profits. However, other industries are almost incapable of breaking a product up into feature groups. Take software. It can be very difficult to break down a product into smaller parts and ask what the value for each is, meaning, how much would customers be willing to pay for each part. Nonetheless, software development teams constantly add features and improve older ones. Over time, the cost of supporting them can far outweigh the return. In recent years, more and more companies are tracking what features are used to help them determine where to invest and what features to drop.

This is important because it allows you to direct the energy of the company toward what customers are willing to pay for.

In thinking about optimization, you need to consider both products and features. Otherwise, you may spend most of your time supporting functionalities that do not add value for customers. And even worse, you lose out spending time innovating and moving your product forward. It is easy to get lost when spending all your time developing new features, testing, and dealing with last-minute problems before shipping. Adding an ROI exercise may be too much. But ignoring it may lead to total product failure. Don't become a dinosaur.

Stakeholders

Almost every for-profit company will want to grow revenue and marketshare. However, a nonprofit organization may be limited by the community it serves, and may be more focused on the quality of their services instead of growth. In all cases, a company will have stakeholders. Stay in tune with them. Pending where you look from, you will have different stakeholders. If you are the CEO, then your stakeholders are the board and your shareholders. If you manage a group in a larger organization, your stakeholders may be the CEO and the executive staff. Regardless, the questions are the same: What do they expect? What are their values? Have they recently changed in any way? Is there a sharper focus on revenue? Is their core belief solving customer problems or finding an exit strategy?

While working at Apple, I saw several major changes in stakeholder value. For many troubling years the company was shrinking. It was a time of survival. Revenue took the lead as being the most important thing. Heroes were born. As a result, the company ended up with more than ten similar computer product lines. The CEO at the time was John Sculley. When he left, Michael Spindler took over. Almost immediately, there was no focus on research and development. All talk was about how to save the company and who would buy it. For a brief time, Gil Amelio came on board as CEO and tried to instill good software development practices while cutting cost. But to no avail. When Steve Jobs took over, it changed again. He clearly said, "We are not cutting cost; we are not letting employees go. Instead we will invest in products that customers will love." He himself took the lead in developing a new computer—the iMac—in record time. After nine months of intense focus on research and development, the iMac shipped. It not only shipped on time, but it followed the existing internal development process and met every milestone along the way. And once it shipped, the number of problems reported by customers was less than half as compared to other Mac computers. The message was loud and clear: great products matter!

Early on at Adobe, deep technical science was a core value instilled by its founders. The company took pride in solving difficult problems. As a result, the company was able to create whole industries around PDFs, fonts, photos, and graphics. The engineering community was given time and encouragement to become industry leaders. Later on, when the founders handed over the day-to-day running of the company, the board and the new executive staff started to focus more on revenue growth. This allowed heroes to be born. Chasing problems that hindered revenue growth became the norm. The engineering community was turned into a resource pool that could be applied to any problem. This resulted in a reduced ability for new science to take hold. The stakeholder value had shifted from deep science to deploying services and features driving new revenue growth.

Different stakeholders have different values. You cannot be successful as a company unless everyone is aligned around these values. Therefore, it is important for leaders to share them, and for employees to understand them.

Employees

Are all employees engaged? Do they have the required skillset and tools? Are they spending time on the right things? Too much focus on time-tracking and writing status reports? Not enough sharing? Are you hiring too quickly? Are too many employees leaving?

There is an endless list of questions to ask. As a leader, it is your responsibility to keep asking questions and deciding on remedies. The goal is to identify opportunities to make employees more effective. In return, they will be happier and more satisfied with their ability to positively influence the company direction.

An important lens for assessing employee contribution is to ask them, "Do you feel that you are contributing to the success of the company? If no, what is preventing you?" Often, the answer is organizational barriers. Groups are too busy catching up from the last late delivery to engage with others, and therefore, closing down new opportunities. A good leader will then think about creating an environment where there is time and space for a group to allow others to contribute. In other words, make building a great product a priority by engaging as many people as possible.

Partners

Are you leveraging your partners' skillsets? What could they do better? Can they do more in certain areas? Are you doing tasks that partners could do better? These are not only questions to ask in areas such as IT. This could be applied in every area of the company. If you don't want to hand over a complete function, they could step in and support when your own capacity is reached.

Buy versus build is an ongoing struggle for many companies. But it is important to keep this option open, especially in areas that are not considered your key competences. It is easy to convince yourself that dominance in one area leads to dominance in another. Very often, transference of skills and success takes much longer than planned. A better answer to the buy versus build could be to do both. Start small with a buy, learn, and then build.

While working at Apple, "ease of use" was a one of the core company beliefs. It was the reason for its existence. Revenue growth was secondary. Even in the midst of a crisis, the focus was not on reducing the size of the organization, but rather on building great products. In order to focus more on innovation rather than upgrading older products, this belief led to the desire to move traditional tasks from internal engineering to our partners. At the time, Apple had all manufacturing done by partners. They also supported minor upgrades. The new goal was to allow Apple engineers to have more time thinking about the next big thing. Hence, we started to move responsibilities to our partners. We defined a joint development model initiative with clear goals on what percentage of the total hardware development effort for a given product should move to our partners by what time. In less than a year, about a quarter of the total effort was moved. Increased investment in innovation, and new products, was achieved by leveraging the current set of partners.

Managing Optimization

As you identify new opportunities to do better, do not fix every one. Do not start new pet initiatives outside of the operational model. Go back to chapter four and carefully update your plan for how to manage the company directions.

Once the operational model is in place, continuously evaluate the ROI of all elements of the company. If needed, update the company directions.

7

Beyond Directions

As a leader of an organization or company, trust your employees and your operational model. Take a step back and become a gardener—plant, water, and weed. It sounds easy, but if this is a new role for you, it will take some time to adjust. It requires new skills and a different way of interacting with employees. It is about letting go and allowing others to step into leadership roles. It may be painful to see them trying and perhaps doing things differently than what you prefer. Becoming a gardener takes patience.

However, there is one more thing a successful gardener must do. And that it is to look ahead for potential new opportunities or catastrophes on the horizon. You are looking for signs of something that is not here yet, something that can grow into a new challenge or opportunity. Is there a cold front coming? Is torrential rain possible? Is there a drought and water supplies will be reduced? Is the soil losing its nutrients for future seasons? Are there new tomato plants that grow faster and taste better? Is the price of your current crop predicted to drop next season? Is there a new crop that doubles the return? The list could be endless.

It is easy to get caught in the day-to-day demands of an organization. There will always be situations where you, the leader, should step in and address problems. You probably have a long list of people who go straight to you for answers. You feel obligated to take care of your organization whenever you see a problem. This is normal. But ask yourself this question: Who should be looking ahead? Is there anyone else better suited for this task?

As a leader you are responsible for creating a vision and steering the company toward this vision. But you are also responsible for removing obstacles and finding better paths. An organization not distracted by a constant string of surprises will move faster toward the vision. Therefore, it is important that you, as a leader, delegate many of the day-to-day tasks. Over time, the new owners of these tasks will probably become as good as you in resolving problems. Your role is to support them in the learning process.

Not looking ahead will eventually destroy the organization. Nothing lasts forever. The world will change. What once was the best idea will fade. New ideas are required to stay ahead. I don't think I have to point out the many companies that have failed by not recognizing the changing trends in their industry. And this is probably the most important reason why a leader must look ahead. The cost of not doing so is catastrophic.

There are many ways of peeking into the future. Information may emerge from your daily interactions with employees or customers, or it may come from competitive analysis or studying market trends. It may come from anywhere. The most important part of looking ahead is to *always* look ahead. Everything new should be filtered through the lens of "could this information make a difference?" Much will not, but some will. A leader who identifies pivotal information ahead of others will be more successful.

Black, purple, and blue are ways of looking for roadblocks or opportunities. Black is about what can go wrong. Purple is about how to become remarkable at what you do. Blue is about something new, something that can give the company a new opportunity with no or little competition.

Black

There are many colors in the rainbow, but black is not one of them. It is the absence of color that makes everything black. As you look ahead, you should think about what would happen if some of your assumptions did not hold true. What if the market is actually half the size of what was originally scoped? What if a new player enters the market and you have no response? How can you stay ahead of those events? An endless number of events could occur. If you can, try to identify and rank them in order of impact and likelihood of occurrence.

If possible, build defenses into your model. What does that mean? For a software company, one approach to reducing risk around changing market conditions or customer demands is to make your development cycle as short as possible. It does not mean you have to release faster because you can. It means you have the ability to do so if needed.

When working at Adobe, the company delivered major updates to its products once per year. It took some product teams up to six months to release the product after they stopped adding new features. Their test cycles were long. Their automated tests did not cover all features. Their build process was slow. The number of software defects that were kept open required a lot of time and effort to manage. The overhead of planning and tracking these defects was huge. As a result there was just a short window of time when new features could be accepted into the product development cycle. Over time, Adobe had ended up with a delivery approach that was very slow at reacting to customer demands.

This worked reasonably well for the company for many years. However, as the industry became more competitive, the demand for new features, new solutions grew. You can solve this challenge by building a development model that can deliver more frequently. You place demands on every part of the model. You make test automation better. You ensure you can build your software in hours, not days or weeks. You set targets for how many open defects any one team is allowed to have. If they exceed that target, they stop all new feature development and start resolving defects. The list goes on.

The result is that you now have a system that can react to new demands because the technical debt is small and you can develop and deliver new features faster. Do you release more frequently? You can, but you don't have to. Warning: what does happen in most cases is that teams release as often as they can, because they want to fix defects. But that is not necessarily what the customers want. The product teams should carefully evaluate the release frequency balancing the cost of releasing, customer benefits, and revenue growth.

In the case of Acrobat, the team developed a sophisticated release strategy to manage the impact on their customers. They would plan one major release per year. That allowed them to provide a good reason for customers to buy or upgrade the product every year. They would also do quarterly updates for critical fixes or a handful of customer-demanded features. They would provide the updates for the current and the past two major releases of Acrobat. In addition, they had a zero-day (within days) patch approach that enabled them to release critical, mostly security-related, bug fixes for any supported Acrobat product.

Another approach for reducing risk is not to commit all your resources to a fixed plan. The world changes. It is simply not possible to foresee what will happen. So allow teams to commit part of their time to a plan, and trust them to make their own decisions on how to spend the rest of their time. Of course, the assumption is that they will spend that time on what is most important to meet the team goals. This is why variants of agile development are becoming the norm in the software development industry.

How do you manage your more mature products? As they become less profitable, there is often increased pressure to keep up with sales projections. It is very common for sales groups to make commitments to improve product lines that are at the tail end of their supported time period. In other words, they sell a product with promises to support it after the engineering organization is already committed to developing a new product. This, of course, results in engineering being held back from spending time on newer, more profitable products.

How do you reconcile the gap? You have many choices here. For software development, you can build up a separate group that fixes and improves already-shipped products, or you can set aside effort in the development organization to fix shipped products. But there are also choices that are less costly, but require more discipline. You can, for example, make the update and patch process consistent across all products, making it less costly to release a patch. Alternatively, you can provide an upgrade to a newer product for free, or at a very reduced cost. Of course, this is much more difficult in larger companies as their environments are more complex and they are more sensitive to the impact of new products, updates, and patches.

Another approach is to strive to make everything you ship compatible with every prior version, making it easier to mix and match product versions. Yes, there are times when this is not possible, but you can strive to make that the exception rather than the norm. You can also test your own stuff. Make it work. Make everything you have work together seamlessly. That is a big task. In larger organizations, this may not be rewarded. What is applauded is the increase in sales for an individual product. If everything you ship is working well with each other, it is much simpler to help customers by sending them the latest version of your product, rather than fixing older products they have installed.

Another black question is: Are you in the right business? Have you defined your business around products or customers? Consider the railroad industry. They did not run into financial problems because of reduced growth in passenger and freight transportation. In fact, transportation demand grew. The railroads did have some federal regulation to overcome, but the main reason for their financial troubles was because of their focus on the railroad rather than on transportation. They had picked a product to be their business instead of customers who had transportation needs. This limited their options in trying to get out of trouble. They did not spend time looking into how to expand or partner in order to make transportation easier. Instead, they spent time on trains and railroads. It can be difficult to separate from a product that helped build American society—an industry that had been successful for more than one hundred years. But there is only one jury of company success: the customer.

Black is about what can go wrong. It is also about how you can prepare by building defenses into your company. Should something go wrong, you are prepared, can avoid panic, and reduce negative impact.

Purple

When looking at the horizon, there is an interesting concept called the "purple cow." It comes from a book of the same name written by Seth Godin. It was groundbreaking when it first came out but has since gotten some criticism. Regardless, the part of the book I really like is that if you have a choice of focus within your field, then pick an area and become really good at it. For example, if you open a law practice, should you do a general practice or focus on a particular topic? Of course, it depends upon the situation, but if you have choice, the book suggests that you should become the best at one subject matter. This approach will make you more successful than anybody else because that is the only thing you do. Over time, you are doing this better than anyone else. As a result, you stand out. Among a field of brown cows, you become the purple cow, the one that stands out.

How does this approach apply to leading an organization? It is about portfolio management. Are you investing in a large number of different technologies or products? Are you spreading your organization too thin? Are you staffing what matters so the important projects can be successful? One common assumption made in software development companies is to assume that all software is the same. It is not. Being good at one programming language in a particular domain does not mean that this knowledge can be transferred to a new domain. For example, knowing how to build photo applications for use on desktop computers does not mean that the same team can do well creating movie applications for iPhones. Sometimes leaders assume that this is an easy transition that can be done in weeks. It is not. It takes time.

These are the core questions: What are you good at? What capabilities does the organization have? Are you investing in these core capabilities? Are you investing in totally new areas that take a while to master? My experience with portfolio management is that investing in areas you know well has a higher probability of success. Investing in many new areas significantly lowers chances of success. Introducing many new variables into an organization increases the probability of failure. Asking an organization simultaneously to learn about new markets, new customers, new distribution channels, new technologies, new *anything*, is more risky than changing one or two things.

Purple is about focusing your portfolio in areas that are best set up for success. Expansion into new areas can be done by following the approach outlined by Jim Collins in his book *Great by Choice*. He says that weak leaders rely on cannonballs, while strong leaders first use bullets. During challenging times it is tempting to look for big, easy, and visible solutions— fire a cannonball. However, it is far wiser to take many small test steps— fire bullets—before making a big change. It is cheaper to test your assumptions by using bullets. It is easier to set up smaller projects to validate your assumptions than it is to implement a whole new solution. Once you have validated a big new idea, then fire a cannonball. And if you can, make it purple.

Blue

The premise of the book *Blue Ocean Strategy*, written by W. Chan Kim and Renée Mauborgne, is that blue oceans refer to industries not yet in existence, the unknown market space. The assumption is that value and demand is out there. The game is to unlock this demand by creating new value. You must reach beyond existing demand. If you can do it, there is a potential for a company to grow and prosper. And as there is no competition, you can set the rules of the game.

Finding *Blue Ocean*, or creating value innovation, is what we all are striving for. Every new start-up promises a blue (or purple) future. There is a limitless supply of new ideas that have yet to be validated. So how do you find the elusive liquid? By trying…your way. Look at what you are doing today and start asking questions. Are these the right goals? Am I focused on real customer demand? Is there something else? Something nearby? One simple way of getting into the *blues* is to hold "blue sessions." Get your teams together. Remind them of the current goals set to achieve the future state of the organization or the company. Then ask: Are these the right goals? Are there better goals that will lead to better outcomes? Are the current assumed customer needs not the right ones? Is there something else they crave?

Consider the iPod. It allowed you to take your whole music library with you anywhere. Was that a demand articulated by customers? No. At the time, you had the ability to play music while moving. And for the most part, that meant bringing a few CDs with you. When the price for the early iPods was announced, Apple was faced with much criticism. Who would pay that much for a portable music player? But it turned out that it was not only a portable music player. It was a device that was sleek, easy to use, and could hold your entire music library. It enabled you to play music anywhere you would go. Biking, running, you name it. This was a game changer. The early sales grew beyond even the most positive of predictions because it created new value.

Beyond Directions

By using the approach outlined in this book, your organization will transform itself to meet any demand you can place upon it. It takes a few iterations before change kicks in. But once it does, it will propel the organization forward. It is a thing of beauty to see a great operational model at work. You can recognize the impact it has anywhere in the company.

It is enormously satisfying to know that it is possible for an organization to operate in a transparent and fully understood way. It enables everyone to put his or her best foot forward toward a common goal. It is not a question of where you are starting this transformation, but rather one of your desire to learn and improve. This is what makes you successful. You may be behind today, but by tomorrow, your steps toward the future will allow you to surpass anyone standing still, resting upon their past successes. A great operational model is a thing of beauty. It propels the company toward a better future.

The most important task for a leader is to look ahead. Black, purple, and blue are lenses that can help you avoid catastrophes and identify new opportunities.

Realize your vision by setting directions!

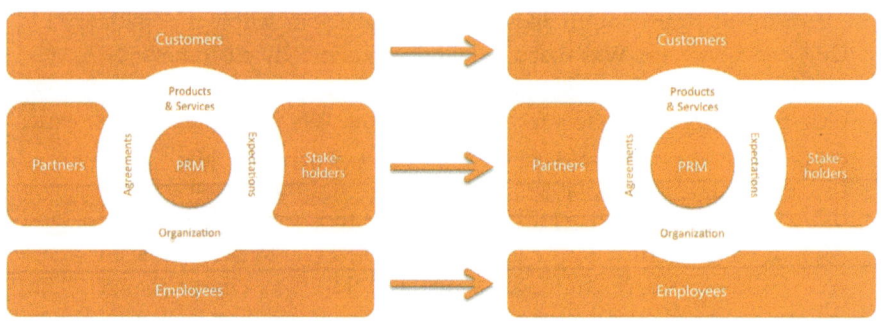

ABOUT THE AUTHOR

Erik Boe currently works at VMware, where he defines and implements software delivery models. Prior to that, he worked at Adobe, where he was part of a global technology group delivering solutions to all Adobe product teams. This central and unique position enabled him to gain deep insight into technology portfolio management and innovation across the company. Before joining Adobe, he was with a start-up struggling to deliver Internet storage solutions. He started his career with Apple. He was there before, during, and after the turnaround, first in the Mac OS group and later in the hardware division. He had roles ranging from software engineer to manager and program manager, driving company-wide efforts focused on optimizing technology delivery and innovation.

He has a master's in international business from Pepperdine University and a bachelor of computer science from the University of California, Santa Barbara.

He grew up in Norway and later moved to California to join the personal computer revolution. He currently lives in California with his wife, three children, a dog, and a cat.

www.ingramcontent.com/pod-product-compliance
Lightning Source LLC
Chambersburg PA
CBHW040811200526
45159CB00022B/275